Customer Service: 1-877-277-9441 or CustomerService@PhoenixInternational.com

Published by PI Kids, an imprint of Phoenix International Publications, Inc.

8501 West Higgins Road	34 Seymour Street	Heimhuder Straße 81
Chicago, Illinois 60631	London W1H 7JE	20148 Hamburg

PI Kids is a trademark of Phoenix International Publications, Inc., and is registered in the United States.

www.PhoenixInternational.com

Library of Congress Control Number: 2024952654

ISBN: 979-8-7654-1206-0

Around the Sun

Our Solar System

Written by Erin Rose Wage
Illustrated by Amy Zhing

pi kids®
An imprint of PHOENIX International Publications, Inc.
Chicago • London • Hamburg • Mexico City • Sydney

Mercury

Eight planets go around the sun.
Rocky **Mercury** is the smallest one.

Venus

Planet **Venus** is the next to spot.
It has volcanoes and it's superhot!

Earth

Earth is the third planet. You are here,
on our cozy blue-green sphere.

Mars

Look out for **Mars**. It's straight ahead!

This rocky planet is rusty red.

Asteroid belt

The **asteroid belt** is next on the list.

It's filled with rocks and a dusty mist.

Jupiter

Gassy **Jupiter** wins the prize

for the planet that is the BIGGEST size!

Saturn

Planet **Saturn** is wrapped with rings,

made of rocks and frozen things.

Uranus

Planet **Uranus** rotates on its side,

taking its rings for a sideways ride!

Neptune

Planet **Neptune**'s winds blow strong,
through days so short and years so long.

Pluto

Dwarf planet **Pluto** is on the run,
spinning out far from the sun!